WHY DID THE CHICKEN CROSS THE ROAD?

WHY DID THE CHICKEN CROSS THE ROAD?

AND OTHER RIDDLES OLD AND NEW

COMPILED BY
JOANNA COLE
AND
STEPHANIE CALMENSON

ILLUSTRATED BY
ALAN TIEGREEN

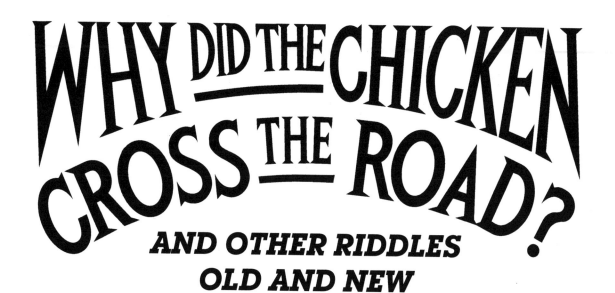

Morrow Junior Books / New York

1 2 3 4 5 6 7 8 9 10

Library of Congress Cataloging-in-Publication Data

Cole, Joanna.
Why did the chicken cross the road?: and other riddles old and new / Joanna Cole
and Stephanie Calmenson; illustrated by Alan Tiegreen.
p. cm.
ISBN 0-688-12202-7 (trade)—ISBN 0-688-12203-5 (library)
1. Riddles, Juvenile. 2. Wit and humor, Juvenile. (1. Riddles. 2. Jokes.)
I. Calmenson, Stephanie. II. Tiegreen, Alan, ill.
PN6371.5.C597 1994 818'.5402—dc20 94-2582 CIP AC

CONTENTS

ABOUT RIDDLES — 6

Why Did the Jelly Roll? — 8

What Do You Call a Baby Whale? — 10

The 2,000-Pound Gorilla — 12

Sherlock Bones — 20

Pooched Eggs on Toast — 22

What Bow Can't Be Tied? — 24

Oldies and Newies — 26

What Did Delaware? — 30

Why Did the Computer Go to the Doctor? — 32

Why Did the Silly-Billy Sit on the Clock? — 34

Worse and Worse — 36

What Time Is It? — 37

A...B...C — 38

Mother Goose Riddles — 42

One, Two, Three — 44

Why Did the Baker Quit His Job? — 46

What Did the Pencil Say to the Paper? — 48

What Color Was Washington's White Horse? — 50

What's the Difference...? — 54

Flip, Flop, Fleezy — 56

What Goes Z-Z-U-B, Z-Z-U-B? — 58

Did You Hear the One About...? — 59

How Did the Tree Say Good-bye? — 60

WHERE TO FIND MORE — 63

SUBJECT INDEX — 64

ABOUT RIDDLES

I have an apple I cannot cut,
A blanket I cannot fold,
And so much money I cannot count it.

This is a riddle that was told long, long ago. The first riddles, say folklorists, go far back in human history. They were not necessarily funny. Rather, they were a way of looking at the world. They showed how two things that seem different on the surface are actually alike in some way. Many were about nature and the universe, and often they were more like poems than jokes.

The answer to the riddle above is: the moon, which is round like an apple; the sky, which is large and flat like a blanket; and the stars, which are scattered through the heavens like sparkling coins.

Other old riddles were matters of life and death. In the mythology of ancient Greece, a dragonlike creature called the Sphinx sat outside the city of Thebes and asked this riddle of everyone who passed:

What walks on four legs in the morning,
two legs at noon, and three legs at night?

Those who couldn't answer were killed by the Sphinx. Finally a man named Oedipus solved the riddle and destroyed the Sphinx. The answer he gave was: man, who crawls on all fours as a baby, walks on two feet as a man, and uses a cane in old age.

Riddles have changed a lot over the years. Now they are told mostly to amuse. The humor comes from playing with language, from taking advantage of the fact that one word often has two or more meanings. Your life may never depend on knowing the answers to the riddles in this book, but we hope they'll make you laugh.

Here is a riddle we'd like to close with:

Why did the pig keep turning around when he read this introduction?

He was looking for the end.

And here it is. . .

The End

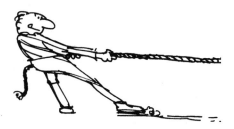

WHY DID THE JELLY ROLL?

Sink your teeth into these funny food riddles.

What did the astronaut cook in his skillet?

Unidentified frying objects.

Why did the jelly roll?

Because it saw the apple turnover.

What's the best thing to put into a chocolate cake?

Your teeth.

How do you make a hamburger roll?
Take it to the top of a hill and give it a push.

How do you make a hot dog stand?
Take away its chair.

How do you make a lemon drop?
Let go of it.

How do you make a strawberry shake?
Put it in the fridge.

How do you make an ice cream pop?
Stick a pin in it.

WHAT DO YOU CALL A BABY WHALE?

Here are some silly ways to describe things.

What do you call two bananas?

A pair of slippers.

What do you call a sick alligator?

An illigator.

What do you call a baby whale?

A little squirt.

What do you call a bee who hums very quietly?

A mumblebee.

What do you call a pony with a sore throat?

A little hoarse.

What do you call a freight train loaded with bubble gum?

A chew-chew train.

What do you call someone who carries an encyclopedia in his pocket?

Smarty-pants.

THE 2,000-POUND GORILLA

He thinks these animal riddles are funny.
So start laughing.

Which side of a chicken has the most feathers?

The outside.

What do you call a 2,000-pound gorilla?

Sir.

What dog says "meow"?

A police dog working undercover.

Where do sheep get their hair cut?

At the baa-baa shop.

What is the best way to keep a skunk from smelling?

Hold his nose.

What do you call a black-and-blue Tyrannosaurus rex?

A dino-sore.

What happened to the cat who swallowed a ball of yarn?

She had mittens.

MORE ANIMAL RIDDLES

How do you know carrots are good for your eyes?

You never see a rabbit wearing glasses.

What is the best way to catch a squirrel?

Climb up a tree and act like a nut.

Why is it hard to talk with a goat around?

He keeps butting in.

Why don't ducks tell jokes while they're flying?

They might quack up.

**Why does a mother kangaroo
hope it doesn't rain?**

She hates it when the children have to play inside.

What did the boy octopus say to the girl octopus?

I want to hold your hand, hand, hand, hand, hand, hand, hand, hand.

**There were ten cats in a boat and one jumped out.
How many were left?**

None. They were copycats.

STILL MORE ANIMALS!

What do rhinoceroses have that no other animal has?

Baby rhinoceroses.

How do you keep a bull from charging?

Take away his credit card.

What does a vet keep outside his front door?

A welcome mutt.

What do you call a cow who works for a gardener?

A lawn mooer.

Why are fish so smart?

Because they live in schools.

How do baby birds learn to fly?

They wing it.

Why do bees hum?

Because they can't remember the words.

What was the turtle doing on the highway?

About one mile an hour.

AND DON'T FORGET THE ELEPHANT RIDDLES

Who is beautiful
and gray and wears
glass slippers?

Cinderelephant.

Why do elephants paint their toenails red?

So they can hide in the strawberry patch.

Why did the elephant sit on the marshmallow?

To keep from falling into the cocoa.

**What time is it when
the elephant
sits on the park bench?**

Time to get a new bench.

How can you tell if there's been an elephant in your refrigerator?

You can see his footprints in the butter.

What's the difference between an elephant and a grape?

The grape is purple.

What is gray and has four legs and a trunk?

A mouse going on vacation. (Fooled you!)

SHERLOCK BONES

Do you have time for some spooky riddles?
Better check your witch watch.

What did Dracula say when he got a present?

"Fangs a lot."

Why did the teacher send Dracula, Jr., home from school?

He was coffin too much.

How did the monster count to one hundred?

On his fingers.

What skeleton was a famous detective?

Sherlock Bones.

What do they call a skeleton who won't get out of bed?

Lazybones.

What is a monster's favorite breakfast cereal?

Scream of wheat.

What is a ghost's favorite kind of music?

Haunting melodies.

How did the witch babies get switched at birth?

It was hard to tell witch was witch.

What did the mother ghoul say to her child when it was raining?

Don't forget your ghoul-ashes.

How is a Cyclops like a pig?

They both have one eye (i) in the middle.

Which monster is a practical joker?

Prankenstein.

POOCHED EGGS ON TOAST

When you cross one thing with another,
you never know what you'll end up with.

What do you get when you cross two dogs, two eggs, and a slice of bread?

Pooched eggs on toast.

What do you get when you cross an elephant with a peanut butter sandwich?

An elephant that sticks to the roof of your mouth or a peanut butter sandwich that never forgets.

What do you get when you cross a rhino with a computer?

A very large know-it-all.

What do you get when you cross a cocker spaniel, a poodle, and a rooster?

A cock-a-poodle-doo.

**What do you get when you
cross a plumber with a jeweler?**

A ring around the bathtub.

**What do you get when you
cross a cat with a laughing hyena?**

A giggle puss.

**What do you get when you
cross a cat with a lemon?**

A sour puss.

**What do you get when you cross a hippo with a
blackbird?**

A lot of broken telephone poles.

What do you get when you cross a parrot with a tiger?

I don't know, but you'd better listen when it talks.

WHAT BOW CAN'T BE TIED?

Things are not always what they seem.

What kind of coat won't keep you warm?

A coat of paint.

What pool is no good for swimming?

A car pool.

What bow can't be tied?

A rainbow.

Which pen won't write?

A pigpen.

When is a door not a door?

When it's ajar.

When is a plane not a plane?

When it's aloft.

When is a bicycle not a bicycle?

When it turns into a driveway.

OLDIES AND NEWIES

Here are some of the oldest, best-known riddles in America, along with some modern versions.

The Fireman's Red Suspenders

The Oldie

Why does the fireman wear red suspenders?

To keep his pants up.

A Newie

Why does the fireman wear blue suspenders?

Because his red ones are in the wash.

Black, White, and Red

The Oldie

What's black and white and red all over?

A newspaper. (Read all over—get it?)

Some Newies

What's black and white and red all over?

A blushing zebra.

What's black and white and red all over?

A sunburned penguin.

MORE OLDIES AND NEWIES

Four Wheels and Flies

The Oldie

What has four legs and flies?

A horse in the summertime.

Some Newies

What has four wheels and flies?

A garbage truck.

What has eight wheels and flies?

A bird on roller skates.

The Chicken and the Road

The Oldie

Why did the chicken cross the road?

To get to the other side.

Some Newies

Why did the chicken cross the road twice?

She was a double-crosser.

Why did the turkey cross the road?

It was the chicken's day off.

WHAT DID DELAWARE?

Is geography funny? Try these riddles and see.

What did Delaware?

She wore her New Jersey.

What did Idaho?

She hoed her Maryland.

What did Tennessee?

She saw what Arkansas.

What state has four eyes but can't see?

Mississippi.

Hiya, hiya, hiya!

Which is the friendliest state?

O-hi-o.

If the green house is on the right side of the road and the red house is on the left side of the road, where is the white house?

In Washington, D.C.

Who should you call when you find Chicago, Ill?

Baltimore, MD.

Can you name the capital of every state in the union in less than fifteen seconds?

Yes, Washington, D.C.

Where do cows go on vacation?

Moo York.

WHY DID THE COMPUTER GO TO THE DOCTOR?

These doctor riddles will have you in stitches.

Why do surgeons wear masks?
So no one will recognize them if they make a mistake.

How did the psychiatrist help the confused pretzel?
She straightened it out.

Why did the boy bring a candy bar to the dentist?
He wanted a chocolate filling.

Why did the clock go to the doctor?
Because it felt run-down.

Why did the umbrella go to the doctor?
It was under the weather.

Why did the computer go to the doctor?
It thought it had a terminal illness.

TELL ME, DOCTOR...

How do you avoid illnesses caused by biting insects?

Don't bite any.

How do you keep from getting a pain in the eye when drinking chocolate milk?

Always take the spoon out of the glass.

How do you keep from getting corns on your toes?

Try planting beans instead.

WHY DID THE SILLY-BILLY SIT ON THE CLOCK?

Nothing is sillier
than a silly-billy riddle.

Why did the silly-billy throw a stick of butter out the window?

He wanted to see a butterfly.

Why did the silly-billy throw a glass of water out the window?

He wanted to see a waterfall.

Why did the silly-billy sit on the clock?

He wanted to be on time.

Why did the silly-billy sit on the television set?

He wanted to be on TV.

Why did the silly-billy tiptoe past the medicine cabinet?

He didn't want to wake the sleeping pills.

YUK - YUK!

Why did the silly-billy tell jokes to his stomach?

He wanted to hear belly laughs.

What showed up when the silly-billy had his head x-rayed?

Nothing.

WORSE AND WORSE
Complaining has never been so funny.

What is worse than a giraffe with a sore throat?
A centipede with sore feet.

What is worse than a centipede with sore feet?
A turtle with claustrophobia.

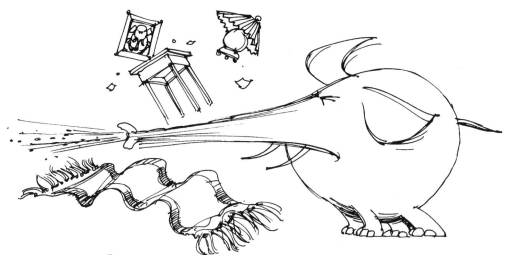

What is worse than a turtle with claustrophobia?
An elephant with hay fever.

WHAT TIME IS IT?

Oh, about five to funny.

What time is it when five grizzly bears are chasing you?

Five after one.

What time is it when you have a toothache?

Tooth-hurty.

What time was it when the baseball team evened the score?

Five to five.

What time is the same spelled backward or forward?

Noon.

Why should you never tell a secret near a clock?

Because time will tell.

A...B...C

There are more letters
in these riddles than there are
in the whole post office.

How many letters are there in the alphabet?

Eleven. T-H-E A-L-P-H-A-B-E-T.

What letters contain nothing?

M-T.

What starts with *T,* ends with *T,* and is filled with *T*?

A teapot.

If Washington went to Washington wearing white woollies while Washington's wife waited in Wilmington, how many *W*'s are there in all?

"There are no *W*'s in "all.""

What ten-letter word starts with *G-A-S*?

Automobile.

MORE LETTER RIDDLES

What word begins with *E,* ends with *E,* and sounds as if it has only one letter in it?

Eye (I).

Spell *we* using two letters other than *W* or *E.*

U and I.

What five-letter word has six left when you take away two letters?

Sixty.

Why is *B* such a hot letter?

It makes oil boil.

Why is honey so scarce in Boston?

Because there is only one B in Boston.

How can you make a witch scratch?

Take away her W.

What letters can climb a wall?

I-V (ivy).

Which are the coldest two letters?

I-C (icy).

MOTHER GOOSE RIDDLES

Take a gander at these riddles from old nursery rhymes. Can you guess what they are about?

Humpty Dumpty sat on a wall.
Humpty Dumpty had a great fall.
All the king's horses
And all the king's men
Couldn't put Humpty together again.

An egg.

Little Nancy Etticoat
With a white petticoat,
And a red nose.
She has no feet or hands,
Yet the longer she stands,
The shorter she grows.

A lighted candle.

As I was going to St. Ives,
I met a man with seven wives.
Each wife had seven sacks,
Each sack had seven cats,
Each cat had seven kits.
Kits, cats, sacks, and wives,
How many were going to St. Ives?

One. (I was the only one going to St. Ives.)

Old Mother Twitchett has but one eye
And a long tail which she lets fly.
And every time she goes over a gap,
She leaves a bit of her tail in a trap.

Needle and thread.

Thirty white horses
Upon a red hill;
Now they tramp,
Now they champ,
Now they stand still.

Teeth and tongue.

ONE, TWO, THREE
Count on these number riddles
to make you laugh.

Why is 6 afraid of 7?

Because 7 8 9.

If a person faints, what number should you bring him?

You should bring him 2.

How many feet in a yard?

It depends how many people are standing in it.

Why is 2 + 2 = 5 like your left foot?

It's not right.

How much is 5 Q plus 5 Q?

10 Q. (You're welcome.)

How many legs does a horse have?

Six. It has forelegs in the front and two legs in the back.

Why is two times ten the same as two times eleven?

Because two times ten equals twenty, and two times eleven equals twenty, too (twenty-two).

WHY DID THE BAKER QUIT HIS JOB?

Do these employees
take their work *seriously*?
What do you think?

How can you tell traffic cops are happy?

They whistle while they work.

Why did the baker quit his job?

He couldn't make enough dough.

How can you tell garbage collectors are sad?

They are often down in the dumps.

Which workers have the best hearing?

Engineers.

What does an attorney wear when he appears in court?

A lawsuit.

What did the author say when they asked her, "How's business?"

"Oh, it's all write."

Why did the mattress salesman get fired?

For lying down on the job.

When are cooks mean?

When they beat the eggs and whip the cream.

Why did the astronaut get the day off?

Because the moon was full.

WHAT DID THE PENCIL SAY TO THE PAPER?

Listen in on these silly conversations.

What did the strawberries say to the farmer?

"Stop picking on me!"

What did the mayonnaise say to the refrigerator?

"Close the door—I'm dressing."

What did the launchpad say to the rocket?

"Can I give you a lift?"

What did the pencil say to the paper?

"I dot my i on you."

What did the beaver say to the tree?

"It's been nice gnawing you."

What did the dirt say to the rain?

"Please stop, or my name will be mud."

What did the lamb say to his mother?

"Thank ewe."

What did one wall say to the other?

"Meet you at the corner."

What did one library book say to the other?

"Can I take you out?"

What did the mother broom say to the baby broom?

"Go to sweep, dear."

WHAT COLOR WAS WASHINGTON'S WHITE HORSE?

Watch out for these tricky riddles!

Antidisestablishmentarianism is the longest word in the English language. How do you spell it?

I-T.

How much dirt is in a hole
six feet long by thirteen feet wide?

None. A hole is empty.

Which weighs more: a pound
of lead or a pound of feathers?

They both weigh a pound.

What color was Washington's white horse?

White.

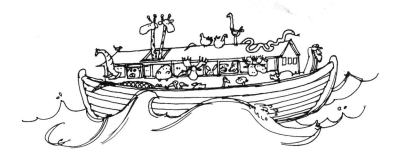

How many animals did Moses take on the ark?

Moses didn't take any animals on the ark. Noah did.

Who can jump higher than a tall building?

Anyone can. Tall buildings can't jump.

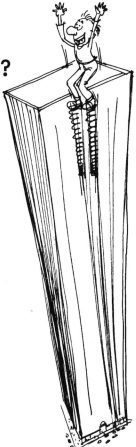

If a rooster laid a white egg and a brown egg, what kinds of chicks would hatch?

None. Roosters don't lay eggs.

Do you say, "Eight and seven *is* thirteen," or "Eight and seven *are* thirteen"?

Neither. Eight and seven equal fifteen.

MORE TRICKY ONES

Why was George Washington buried at Mount Vernon?

Because he was dead.

Who is buried in Grant's tomb?

Ulysses S. Grant.

How many acorns grow on the average pine tree?

None. Pine trees don't have acorns.

Is it better to write on a full stomach or an empty stomach?

It's better to write on paper.

Which would you rather have, an old ten-dollar bill or a new one?

I'd rather have any ten-dollar bill than a new one-dollar bill.

Six children, four adults, and two dogs shared one small umbrella. Who got wet?

No one. It wasn't raining.

How many jelly beans can you put in an empty jelly-bean jar?

Only one. After that the jar isn't empty anymore.

When can you knock over a full glass and not spill any water?

When the glass is full of milk.

If it takes thirteen men eleven days to dig a hole, how long will it take seven men to dig half a hole?

There is no such thing as half a hole.

WHAT'S THE DIFFERENCE...?
Find out in these riddles.

What's the difference between a prizefighter and a man with a cold?

One knows his blows and the other blows his nose.

What's the difference between a counterfeit dollar and a crazy rabbit?

One is bad money and the other is a mad bunny.

What's the difference between a butcher and a light sleeper?

One weighs a steak and the other stays awake.

What's the difference between a teacher and a railway engineer?

One trains the mind and the other minds the train.

What's the difference between a jail warden and a jeweler?

One watches cells and the other sells watches.

What's the difference between a rain gutter and a clumsy outfielder?

One catches drops and the other drops catches.

FLIP, FLOP, FLEEZY

Rhyming riddles were popular in olden days.
See if you can guess these.

Flip, flop, fleezy,
Slippery, wet, and greasy.
When it's out,
It flops about.
Flip, flop, fleezy.

Fish.

Four stiff-standers,
Four dilly-danders,
Two lookers,
Two crookers,
And a wig-wag.

Cow.

When it flares up, it does a lot of good.
But when it dies, it's just paper or wood.

Match.

Very nice, very neat,
Has teeth, but cannot eat.

Comb.

Runs all day,
But never runs away.

Clock.

Riddle cum, riddle cum ruckup,
What fell down and stuck up?

Fork.

It wasn't my sister nor my brother,
But still was the child of my father and mother.
Who was it?

Myself.

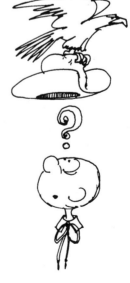

Riddle me, riddle me, what is that
Over the head and under the hat?

Hair.

WHAT GOES Z-Z-U-B, Z-Z-U-B?

Do you hear a strange sound?
Find out what is making it in these noisy riddles!

What goes *abcdefghijklmnopqrstuvwxyz slurp?*

Someone eating alphabet soup.

What goes *99 thump, 99 thump, 99 thump. . . ?*

A centipede with a wooden leg.

What goes *z-z-u-b, z-z-u-b?*

A bee flying backward.

What goes *hoe, hoe, hoe?*

A farmer laughing.

DID YOU HEAR THE ONE ABOUT...?

You haven't heard yet?
Well, here's your chance.

Did you hear the one about the memory contest?
Yes, but I forgot.

Did you hear the one about the skunk?
It stank.

Did you hear the one about the butter?
Please don't spread it around.

Did you hear the one about the pencil?
Yes, I wrote it down.

Did you hear the one about the elevator?
It had its ups and downs.

**Did you hear the one about
the dinosaur egg?**
It cracked me up in a big way.

HOW DID THE TREE SAY GOOD-BYE?

Here are a few fond farewells.

How did the ocean say good-bye?

It waved.

How did the shopper say good-bye?

"Buy-buy."

How did the tree say good-bye?

"Gotta leave."

How did the needle and thread say good-bye?

"Sew long."

How did the eye doctor say good-bye?

How do you say
good-bye to a friend?

Take three letters away,
and that is the end.

wHeRe To FiNd MoRe

SOME SOURCES FOR RIDDLES

Beisner, Monika. *Book of Riddles*. New York: Farrar, Straus & Giroux, 1983.

Brandreth, Gyles. *The Big Book of Silly Riddles*. New York: Sterling Publishing, 1987.

Calmenson, Stephanie. *101 Silly Summertime Jokes*. New York: Scholastic, 1989.

Cole, Joanna, and Stephanie Calmenson. *The Laugh Book*. New York: Doubleday, 1986.

Emrich, Duncan. *The Whim-Wham Book*. New York: Four Winds, 1975.

Keller, Charles. *Colossal Fossils: Dinosaur Riddles*. New York: Simon & Schuster, 1991.

Leach, Maria. *Riddle Me, Riddle Me, Ree*. New York: Viking Press, 1970.

Morrison, Lillian, ed. *Black Within and Red Without*. New York: Thomas Y. Crowell, 1953.

Phillips, Louis. *Haunted House Jokes*. New York: Viking Penguin, 1987.

Rosenbloom, Joseph. *The Biggest Riddle Book in the World*. New York: Sterling Publishing, 1976.

Tashjian, Virginia. *Juba This and Juba That*. Boston: Little, Brown, 1969.

Thaler, Mike. *Funny Side Up! How to Create Your Own Riddles*. New York: Scholastic, 1985.

Withers, Carl. *A Rocket in My Pocket: The Rhymes and Chants of Young Americans*. New York: Henry Holt, 1988.

SUBJECT INDEX

alphabet, letters of, 38–41, 45,
    50, 58, 61
animals, 10–19, 22–23, 36, 37,
    48, 51
  bird, 17, 23, 27, 28
  cat, 13, 15, 23, 43
  chicken, 12, 22, 29, 51
  cow, 16, 31, 56
  dinosaur, 13, 59
  elephant, 18–19, 22, 36
  fish, 17, 56
  horse, 11, 28, 43, 45, 50
  insect, 11, 17, 28, 33, 36, 58
  rabbit, 14, 54
  sheep, 13, 49
  skunk, 13, 59
  turtle, 17, 36

body, parts of, 33, 35, 43, 44,
    52, 57
book, 49
building, parts of, 25, 49, 59

clock, 32, 34, 37, 57
clothing, 11, 24, 26
colors, 27, 50

family members, 49, 57
famous people, 20, 39, 50–52
farewells, 60–62
food, 8–9, 48
  bread, 22
  butter, 34, 59
  dessert, 8, 9, 18, 32
  eggs, 22, 42
  fruit, 9, 10, 19, 23, 48

  peanut butter, 22
  vegetables, 14, 33
  water, 34, 53

geography, 30–31

illness, 10, 32, 33, 36, 37, 44,
    54

money, 52, 54

numbers, 15, 44–45, 50–53, 58
nursery rhymes, 42–43

professions, 46–47, 54–55
  astronaut, 8, 47
  dentist, 32
  doctor, 32, 61
  farmer, 48, 58
  fireman, 26
  jeweler, 23, 55
  plumber, 23
  veterinarian, 16

scary creatures, 20–21, 41
silly-billy, 34–35
sports, 24, 37, 54, 55

television, 34
time, 34, 37
transportation, 11, 24, 25, 28,
    48
tree, 52, 61

weather, 49, 53
writing, 24, 47, 48, 52, 59